the LOONIEST LIMERICK BOOK in the WORLD

by
JOSEPH ROSENBLOOM
ILLUSTRATIONS by SANFORD HOFFMAN

 Sterling Publishing Co., Inc. New York

Books by Joseph Rosenbloom

Bananas Don't Grow on Trees
Biggest Riddle Book in the World
Daffy Definitions
Doctor Knock-Knock's Official Knock-Knock
  Dictionary
Funny Insults & Snappy Put-Downs
Gigantic Joke Book
How Do You Make an Elephant Laugh?
Looniest Limerick Book in the World
Mad Scientist
Monster Madness
Official Wild West Joke Book
Polar Bears Like It Hot
Ridiculous Nicholas Haunted House Riddles
Ridiculous Nicholas Pet Riddles
Ridiculous Nicholas Riddle Book
Silly Verse (and Even Worse)
Wacky Insults and Terrible Jokes

Library of Congress Cataloging in Publication Data

Rosenbloom, Joseph.
  The looniest limerick book in the world.

  Includes index.
  Summary: A collection of some of the looniest, best,
worst, oldest, newest, and silliest limericks.
  1. Limericks, Juvenile. [1. Limericks] I. Hoffman,
Sanford, ill. II. Title.
PN6231.L5R67   808.81'7   81-85034
ISBN 0-8069-4660-1   AACR2
ISBN 0-8069-4661-X (lib. bdg.)

ISBN 0-8069-7920-8 (pbk.)

First paperback printing 1984

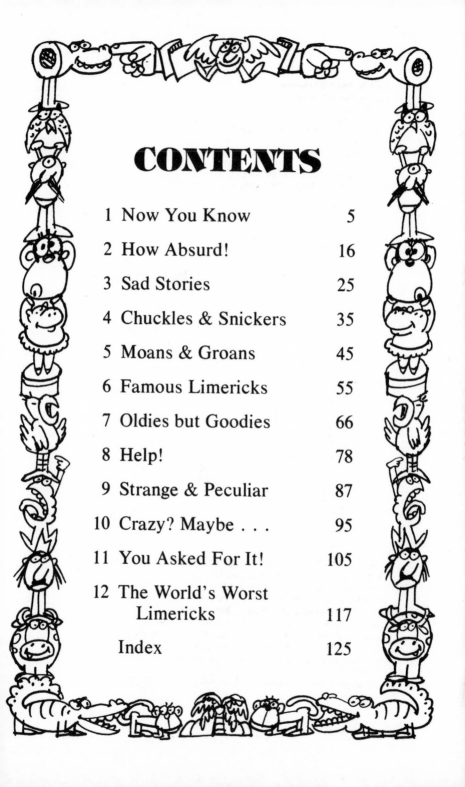

CONTENTS

To Meredith Lynn Backerman
with love

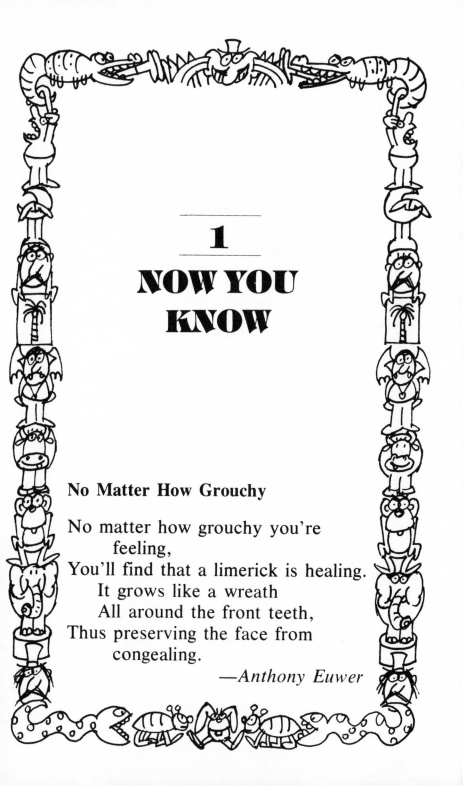

1
NOW YOU KNOW

No Matter How Grouchy

No matter how grouchy you're
    feeling,
You'll find that a limerick is healing.
    It grows like a wreath
    All around the front teeth,
Thus preserving the face from
    congealing.

—*Anthony Euwer*

Too Tight

There was a young lady of Twickenham,
Whose boots were too tight to walk
    quickenham.
    She wore them a while,
    But after a mile,
She pulled them both off and was
    sickenham.

The Star of the Show

Said a rooster, "I want you to know,
I'm really the star of the show.
    The sun—that young pup—
    Wouldn't even get up—
Unless I decided to crow."

Put Them Back, Jack

There was an old fellow of Cosham,
Who took out his false teeth to wash
    'em.
    But his wife said, "Now, Jack,
    If you don't put them back,
I'll jump on those old things and squash
    'em."

Off to the Clink

There once was a sailor named Link,
Whose mates rushed him off to the clink.
    Said he, "I've a skunk
    As a pet in my bunk—
That's no reason for raising a stink."

A Hen in Reading

A hen who resided in Reading,
Attended a gentlemen's wedding.
    As she walked up the aisle,
    The guests had to smile,
In spite of the tears they were shedding.

She Gave One to Adam

A greedy young lady of Eden,
On apples was quite fond of feedin'.
    She gave one to Adam,
    Who said, "Thank you, Madam,"
And then they were kicked out of Eden.

He Had Rough Trousers

There was a man in Atchison,
Whose trousers had rough patchison.
    He found them great,
    He'd often state,
To scratch his wooden matchison.

An Oyster from Kalamazoo

An oyster from Kalamazoo,
Confessed he was feeling quite blue.
    "For," said he, "as a rule,
    When the weather turns cool,
I'm apt to get into a stew."

Wrapped Up His Wife

There was an old widower, Doyle,
Who wrapped up his wife in tinfoil.
    He thought it would please her
    To stay in the freezer—
And, anyway, outside she'd spoil.

He Played the Cello

Said a cellist, a modest young fellow,
When praised for his playing so mellow,
    "It's the easiest thing;
    I just butter each string
With a morsel of strawberry jello."

Collapsed from the Strain

A maiden at college, Miss Keyes,
Weighed down by B.A.'s and M.D.'s,
    Collapsed from the strain.
    Said her doctor, "It's plain
You are killing yourself—by degrees!"

The Great Crocodile

You will find by the banks of the Nile,
The haunts of the great crocodile.
    He will welcome you in
    With an innocent grin—
Which gives way to a satisfied smile.

A Very Strange Lad

A very strange lad from Glas*gow*
Took all of his meals with his cow.
    He explained, "It's uncanny,
    She's so like Aunt Fanny!"
But he didn't indicate how.

A Baby in Kalamazoo

A baby in Kalamazoo
Remarked quite distinctly, "Goo-goo."
    'Twas explained by his ma,
    And likewise his pa,
That he meant to say, "How do you
      do?"

Out in the Kitchen

There was a young lady named Maude,
A very deceptive young fraud.
    She never was able
    To eat at the table,
But out in the kitchen—Oh, Lord!

Sixty-five Eggs

There was a longshoreman named Sid,
Ate sixty-five eggs in Madrid.
    When they asked, "Are you faint?"
    He replied, "No, I ain't,
But I don't feel as well as I did."

Arriving in Heaven

To a person arriving in Heaven,
Said St. Peter, "We dine sharp at seven,
   Then breakfast's at eight—
   Never mind if you're late—
'Cause there's biscuits and milk at
    eleven."

Loved Her Cat

There was a young lady from Burr,
Whose kitten had ultra-thick fur.
    She just loved to stroke it,
    And pat it and poke it,
For the pleasure of hearing it purr.

They Dropped Like Flies

The girl in the Chinese pagoda
Ate onions from fair Minnesota,
    And garlic from Greece
    And Limburger cheese
And her friends dropped like flies from
    the odor.

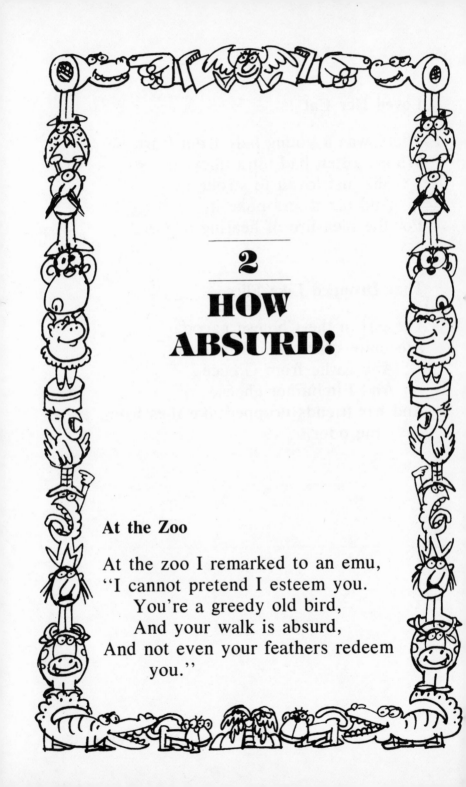

2
HOW ABSURD!

At the Zoo

At the zoo I remarked to an emu,
"I cannot pretend I esteem you.
   You're a greedy old bird,
   And your walk is absurd,
And not even your feathers redeem
   you."

A Silly Giraffe

Jerome was a silly giraffe
Who wore a disguise for a laugh.
    Well, Jerome was too tall
    (or the costume too small).
Did it cover Jerome? Only half!

Sat on His False Teeth

There was an old man of Tarentum,
Who sat on his false teeth and bent 'em.
　　When asked what he lost
　　And how much they cost,
He said, "They're not mine; I just rent
　　'em."

My New Hat

A woman named Mary McGowen
Once said to her old husband, "How in
    The world can I wear
    My new hat to the fair
If you've used it for milking the cow in?"

"Will You Do It Again?"

A boy who played tunes on a comb,
Had become such a nuisance at homb,
    His ma spanked him; then—
    "Will you do it again?"
And he cheerfully answered her,
        "Nomb."

Never Kissed

A grouchy old girl from Tibet,
Had never kissed anyone yet.
    Along came a cat—
    And she said, "I'll kiss that!"
But the cat answered, "Not on a bet!"

Needs Help

There was an old lady of Reading
Who never knew where she was heading.
    She'd start in the east
    On her way to a feast,
And end in the north at a wedding.

Invited Fish

A fellow who lived on the Rhine
Saw some fish on which he wished to
    dine.
    But how to invite them?
    He said, "I will write them!"
He sat down and dropped them a line.

A Cat in the Wings

Of a sudden the great prima donna,
Cried, "Heavens, my voice is a goner!"
    But a cat in the wings
    Said, "I know how she sings,"
And finished the solo with honor.

A Young Russian Named Bowski

There was a young Russian named
    Bowski,
Who called his apartment his howski.
    His gum he called chewski,
    His cow, moo-moo-mooski,
And his little dog,
    bow-wow-wow-wowski.

Held Up and Robbed

Two eager and dashing young beaus
Were held up and robbed of their clothes.
    While the weather is hot,
    They don't mind it a lot,
But what will they do when it snows?

Swam All Alone

There was a young lady named Lee,
Who swam all alone in the sea.
    People said, "You'll be drowned,"
    But she sniffed and she frowned,
And said, "Pish-tosh and fiddle-de-dee!"

A Silly Young Man

A silly young man from Port Clyde
In a funeral procession was spied.
    Asked, "Who is dead?"
    He giggled and said,
"I don't know. I just came for the ride."

Out with a Grasshopper

A young lady timid and proper
Went walking out with a grasshopper.
    When she wanted to stop,
    He continued to hop,
And got home before her to supper.

Said a Crow to a Pelican

Said a crow to a pelican, "Grant
Me the loan of your bill, for my aunt
    Has asked me to tea."
    Said the other, "Not me,
Ask my brother, please, this pelican't!"

A Student Named Dresser

There once was a student named
    Dresser,
Whose knowledge got lesser and lesser.
    It at last grew so small,
    He knew nothing at all;
And now he's a college professor.

Now When She Laughs

An athletic young girl of Papua
Invited a bull to pursue her.
    She vaulted the gate
    Just a fraction too late;
Now when she laughs, she says,
    "Oo-ah!"

3
SAD STORIES

Loch Ness Monster

A visitor once to Loch Ness
Met the monster, who left him
    a mess.
    They returned his entrails
    By the regular mails
And the rest of the stuff by
    express.

An Old Bulldog

There was an old bulldog named Caesar,
Who went for a cat just to tease her;
    But she spat and she spit
    Till the old bulldog quit.
Now when poor Caesar sees her, he flees
    her.

Went for a Sail

There was a young woman named Gail,
Who fancied she'd go for a sail.
    Well, she boarded the yacht,
    But she stayed on her cot,
'Cept when she hung over the rail.

An Odd Fellow from Ecuador

An odd fellow from Ecuador,
Had the same shape behind as before.
    They did not know where
    They should offer a chair,
So he had to sit down on the floor.

An Old Woman of Thrace

There was an old woman of Thrace
Whose nose spread all over her face.
    She got very few kisses;
    The reason for this is
There wasn't a suitable place.

At a Bullfight

At a bullfight in sunny Madrid,
A tourist went clean off his lid.
   He made straight for the bull,
    While the crowd yelled, "The fool
Will go home on a slab!"—and he did.

Two Cats in Kilkenny

There once were two cats in Kilkenny.
Each cat thought there was one too
    many,
    So they scratched and they fit
    And they tore and they bit,
Till instead of two—there weren't any.

But What Can I Do?

Said a gentle old man, "I suppose
I ought not to wear my best clothes.
    But what can I do?
    I have only two,
And these are no better than those."

For Richer or Poorer

There was a young man from Angora
Who married—for richer or poorer.
    He'd not been long wed,
    When he fell out of bed,
And said, "Drat, I have married a
    snorer!"

Died of the Shock

Here lies a young salesman named
    Phipps,
Who married on one of his trips
    A widow named Block.
    He died of the shock
When he saw there were six little chips.

Poor Ben

There was an old puzzler, Ben Ross,
Who died—doing crosswords, of course.
    He was buried, poor Ben,
    With eraser and pen
In a box six feet down, three across.
          —*Sheila Anne Barry*

Higher and Higher

There was a young girl in the choir
Whose voice went up higher and higher.
    It reached such a height,
    It was clear out of sight;
And they found it next day in the spire.

A Young Lady from Niger

There was a young lady from Niger,
Who smiled as she rode on a tiger.
    They came back from a ride
    With the lady inside,
And a smile on the face of the tiger.

Crashed in the Bay

A daring young fellow in Bangor
Sneaked a huge jet from its hangar.
   When he crashed in the bay,
   Neighbors laid him away
Much more in sorrow than anger.

Many an Ounce

A girl who weighs many an ounce,
Used language I will not pronounce,
    When a fellow (unkind)
    Pulled her chair out behind—
He wanted to see if she'd bounce.

In His Hot-Air Balloon

Said young Rex in his hot-air balloon,
"I shall see all the stars very soon."
    Rex was right, for he dropped,
    And he saw when he stopped
Three million bright stars and a moon.

Interrupted Two Girls

A painter who lived in Great Britain,
Interrupted two girls with their knittin'.
    He said with a sigh,
    "That park bench—well, er—I
Just painted it, right where you're
    sittin'."

Carried Politeness Too Far

There was a young girl from Bryn Mawr
Who carried politeness too far.
    "Don't look now," she said,
    With a tilt of her head,
"But someone is stealing your car!"

Paper Trousers

A thrifty young fellow of Shoreham
Made brown paper trousers and
      woreham.
    He looked nice and neat
    Till he bent in the street
To pick up a pin, then he toreham.

One More Crust

A greedy young actress once said,
As she gobbled down slices of bread,
    "If I eat one more crust,
    I'm sure I will bust"—
At which point her audience fled.

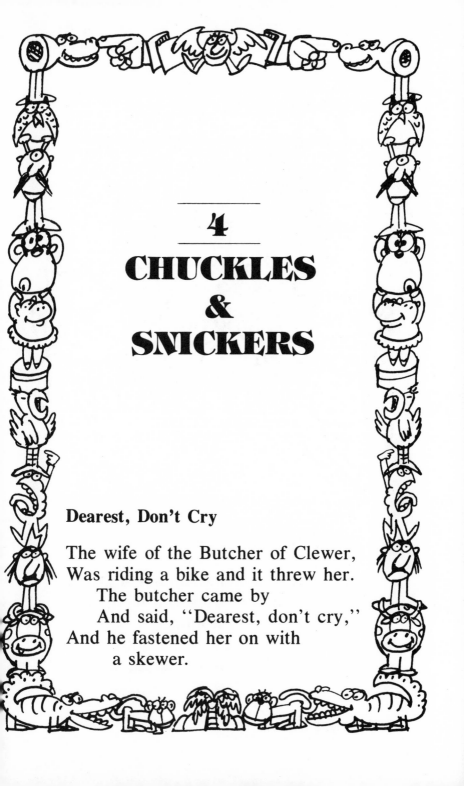

4
CHUCKLES
&
SNICKERS

Dearest, Don't Cry

The wife of the Butcher of Clewer,
Was riding a bike and it threw her.
   The butcher came by
    And said, "Dearest, don't cry,"
And he fastened her on with
    a skewer.

A Sultan Named Darren

There once was a sultan named Darren
Who liked to play tricks on his harem.
    He caught him a mouse
    Which he loosed in the house
And called the result—"harum-scarum!"

Took a Bath Every Day

A man of terrific physique
Took a bath every day in a creek,
    Till one day it ran dry.
    Then he said with a sigh, .
"Call the plumber! This thing's sprung a
    leak!"

Sad to Relate

There was a young maid of Manila,
Whose favorite ice cream was vanilla.
    But sad to relate,
    Though you piled up her plate,
'Twas impossible ever to fill her.

Not Once

There was a young lady of Spain,
Who hiccuped while riding a train,
    Not once, but again
    And again and again,
And again and again and again!

Two Maidens

Two maidens were seated at t.,
Discussing the things that might b.
    "I think I'll wed Willie,"
    Said Mollie to Millie,
"That is, if he asks me, you c."

A Young Lady of Skye

There was a young lady of Skye,
With a shape like a capital "I."
    She said, "It's too bad,
    But then I can pad,"
Which just shows how figures can lie.

A Careless Zookeeper

A careless zookeeper named Blake
Fell into a tropical lake.
    Said a fat alligator,
    A few minutes later,
"That's nice, but I still prefer steak."

A Barber Arose

A clergyman read from his text
How Samson was scissored and vexed.
Then a barber arose
From his sweet summer doze,
Got rattled, and shouted, "Who's next?"

A Young Man So Benighted

There was a young man so benighted,
He never knew when he was slighted.
    He'd go to a party,
    And eat just as hearty
As if he'd been really invited.

Isn't It Odd?

There once was a pretty young thing
Who, when somebody asked her to sing,
    Replied, "Isn't it odd?
    I can never tell 'God
Save the Weasel' from 'Pop Goes the
    King'!"

She Woke in Dismay

There was a young girl named Bianca,
Who slept while the ship lay at anchor.
    She woke in dismay,
    When she heard the mate say,
"Now hoist up the topsheets and
    spanker!"

But I'm Safe

There was an old fellow named Cass
Who had all his pants made of brass.
    When I asked, "Do they chafe?"
    He said, "Yes, but I'm safe
Against pinches, and snakes in the
    grass."

Let Us Pray

The lazy old vicar of Bray
Allowed all his flowers to decay.
    His wife, more alert,
    Bought a powerful squirt,
And said to her spouse, "Let us spray."

A Most Horrible Squint

There was a young lady of Flint,
Who had a most horrible squint.
    She would scan the whole sky
    With her uppermost eye,
While the other was reading small print.

A Canner

A canner, exceedingly canny,
One morning remarked to his granny,
    "A canner can can
    Anything that he can,
But a canner can't can a can, can he?"

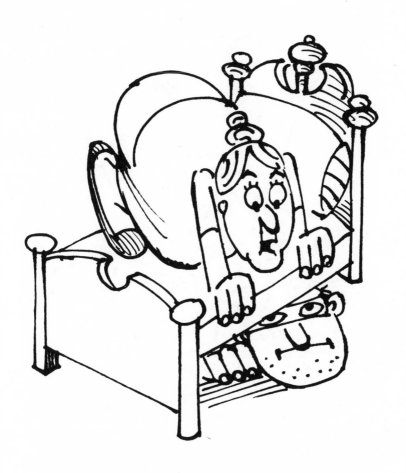

A Kindly Old Lady

A kindly old lady once said,
To a thief she found under her bed,
    "So near to the door,
    And so close to the floor,
I'm afraid you'll catch cold in your
      head."

A Hippo

A hippo from Chesapeake Bay
Decided to take up ballet.
    So she stood on her toes
    And said, "Okay, here goes!"
And she made a big splash—on
    Broadway.

5

MOANS & GROANS

Promises, Promises

In love was poor Elliot Pruitt
With a beautiful girl, but he blew it.
    He said, "I'd die for you, dear,"
    But she said, "Now, look here,
You promise but you never do it."
                —*Sheila Anne Barry*

An Old Lady of Vista

There was an old lady of Vista,
Who vowed that no man ever kissed her.
    But her chin and her nose
    Grew together so close—
That if anyone tried he'd have missed
      her.

Ex-President Taft

They say that ex-President Taft,
When hit by a golf ball, once laughed
    And said, "I'm not sore,
    But although he called 'Fore'
The place where he hit me was aft."

Slipped on a Banana

There was a young girl in Havana
Who slipped on a skin of banana.
    Away went her feet,
    And she took a seat
In a very unladylike manner.

Snored and Snored

An elephant lay in his bunk
In slumber his chest rose and sunk.
　　He snored and he snored,
　　　Till the jungle folks roared—
And his wife tied a knot in his trunk.

Atlas

Despite his impressive physique,
Atlas was really quite meek.
    If a mouse showed its head,
    He would jump into bed,
With a terrible blood-curdling shriek.

Wore a Kettle

A charming old lady named Gretel,
Instead of a hat, wore a kettle.
    When they called her misguided,
    She said, "I've decided
To show all the neighbors my mettle."

A Silly Young Ninny

A fellow who lived in New Guinea
Was known as a silly young ninny.
    He utterly lacked
    Good judgment and tact,
And as for clean socks—hadn't any!

A Young Lady of Cork

There was a young lady of Cork
Whose Pa made a fortune in pork.
    He bought for his daughter
    A tutor who taught her
To balance green peas on her fork.

Kind Little Katy

K is for kind little Katy.
Who weighs near a hundred and eighty!
   She eats ten times a day,
   And her doctors all say
That's the reason she's growing so
    weighty.

So She Cried

There was a fat lady of Clyde
Whose shoelaces once came untied.
   She didn't dare bend
   For fear she'd offend,
So she cried and she cried and she cried.

Only the Tooth

A dentist who lives in Duluth
Had wedded a widow named Ruth,
   Who is so sentimental
   Concerning things dental,
She now utters only the tooth.

A Dentist Named Archibald Moss

A dentist named Archibald Moss
Fell in love with the dainty Miss Ross.
    But he held in abhorrence
    Her name (it was Florence),
And renamed her his Dental Floss.

William John Lew

A fellow named William John Lew
Got more hairy each year as he grew.
    Unable one day
    To shave it away,
He sighed, "Call me Winnie-the-Pooh!"

Mamma Was a Goat

A cheese that was aged and grey
Was walking and talking one day.
    Said the cheese, "Kindly note
    My mamma was a goat
And I'm made out of curds, by the
      whey."

Grape Marmalade

There once was a clever young maid
Who only ate grape marmalade.
    At one hundred and three
    She said with a *WHEE*!
"How nicely preserved I have stayed!"

Next Page!

A newspaper reader named Gage
Would fly into a terrible rage
    When he would choose
    To read some big news
And find it continued . . .
                next page!

The Gorilla's Grimace

The menagerie came to our place,
And I loved the Gorilla's grimace.
   It surprised me to learn
   That he owned the concern,
Being human, but odd in the face.
            —*H. G. Dixey*

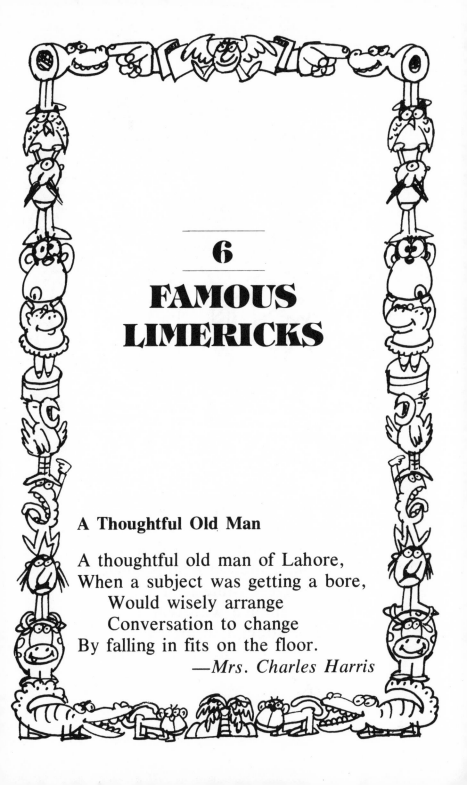

6

FAMOUS LIMERICKS

A Thoughtful Old Man

A thoughtful old man of Lahore,
When a subject was getting a bore,
    Would wisely arrange
    Conversation to change
By falling in fits on the floor.
          —*Mrs. Charles Harris*

An Old Hag of Malacca

There was an old hag of Malacca,
Who smoked such atrocious tobacca,
    When tigers came near,
    They trembled with fear
And didn't attempt to attaca.
                 —Walter Parke

As a Beauty

As a beauty I am not a star,
There are others more handsome by far;
    But my face—I don't mind it,
    For I am behind it;
It's the people in front that I jar.
               —*Anthony Euwer*

Resembled a Pin

There was a young lady so thin
That she closely resembled a pin;
    Don't think that I'd creep
    To the window and peep,
I was told by a friend who looked in.
               —*Gelett Burgess*

There Was An Old Man

There was an old man on whose nose
Most birds of the air could repose;
    But they all flew away
    At the close of the day,
Which relieved that old man and his
      nose.
               —*Edward Lear*

Tut-Ankh-Amen

Tut-Ankh-Amen, best known as old
    Tankh,
Was a Pharaoh of infinite rank;
    But his sarcophagus
    Wouldn't cause all this fuss
If his name had been Freddie or Frank.
              —*Elsie Ridgewell*

Taught Ducklings

There was an old lady of France,
Who taught little ducklings to dance;
    When she said, "Tick-a-tack!"
    They only said, "Quack!"
Which grieved that old lady of France.
              —*Edward Lear*

Well Protected

Oh, I'm glad I'm protected from knocks,
From my necktie clear down to my
    socks,
    And padded and bolstered
    Fenced in and upholstered
With muscles to take up the shocks.
              —*Anthony Euwer*

Three Wives at a Time

There once was an old man of Lyme
Who married three wives at a time.
    When asked, "Why a third?"
    He replied, "One's absurd!
And bigamy, sir, is a crime!"
                 —*Cosmo Monkhouse*

An Important Young Man

An important young man of Quebec
Had to welcome the Duchess of Teck.
   So he bought for a dollar
   A very high collar
To save himself washing his neck.
           —*J. H. Pitman*

I'd Rather Have Fingers

I'd rather have fingers than toes;
I'd rather have ears than a nose;
    And as for my hair,
    I'm glad it's all there:
I'll be awfully sad when it goes.
                    —*Gelett Burgess*

I'd Rather Have Habits

I'd rather have habits than clothes,
For that's where my intellect shows.
    And as for my hair,
    Do you think I should care
To comb it at night with my toes?
                    —*Gelett Burgess*

A Princess of Bengal

There was a princess of Bengal,
Whose mouth was exceedingly small;
    Said she, "It would be
    More easy for me
To do without eating at all!"
                    —*Walter Parke*

A Smell of Gas

Said a foolish young lady of Wales,
"A smell of gas prevails."
    Then she searched with a light
    And later that night
Was collected—in seventeen pails.
                —*Langford Reed*

A Moppsikon Floppsikon Bear

There was an old person of Ware
Who rode on the back of a bear;
    When they said, "Does it trot?"
    He said: "Certainly not,
It's a Moppsikon Floppsikon bear."
                —*Edward Lear*

Funnily Dressed

There once was an old man of Brest,
Who was always funnily dressed:
    Who wore gloves on his nose,
    And a hat on his toes,
And a boot in the middle of his chest.
                —*Cosmo Monkhouse*

This Walking Around

I wish that my room had a floor;
I don't care very much for the door,
    But this walking around
    Without touching the ground
Is getting to be such a bore.

               —Gelett Burgess

You Will Think It Absurd

Said the snail to the tortoise: "You may
Find it hard to believe what I say;
    You will think it absurd,
    But I give you my word,
They fined me for speeding today."

    . . . .

"Well, well!" said the tortoise. "Dear
    me,
How defective your motor must be!
    Though I speed every day
    Not a fine do I pay;
The police cannot catch me, you see!"
                —Oliver Herford

They Came from Oporta

There was once a man from Oporta
Who daily got shorter and shorter,
    The reason he said
    Was the hod on his head,
Which was filled with the heaviest
      mortar.

    . . . .

His sister named Lucy O'Finner
Grew constantly thinner and thinner,
    The reason was plain,
    She slept out in the rain,
And was never allowed any dinner.
            —*Lewis Carroll*

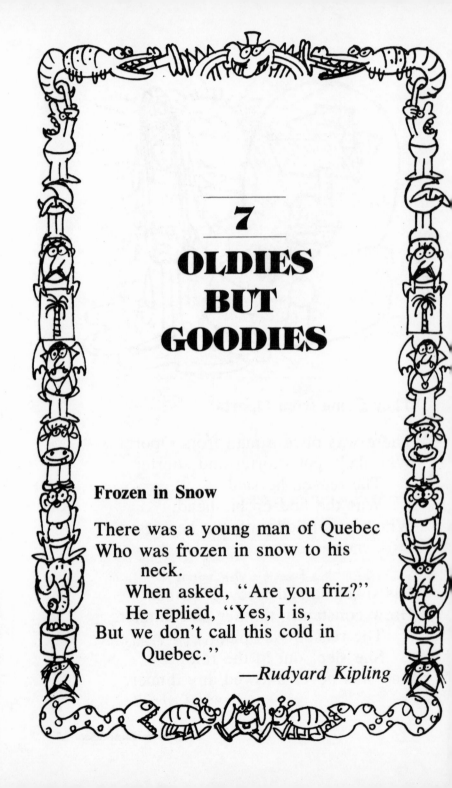

7

OLDIES BUT GOODIES

Frozen in Snow

There was a young man of Quebec
Who was frozen in snow to his
    neck.
    When asked, "Are you friz?"
    He replied, "Yes, I is,
But we don't call this cold in
    Quebec."
                —*Rudyard Kipling*

Is It Harder to Toot?

A tutor who tooted a flute
Tried to teach two young tooters to toot.
   Said the two to the tutor,
   "Is is harder to toot, or
To tutor two tutors to toot?"
           —Carolyn Wells

An Old Man of Dumbree

There was an old man of Dumbree
Who taught little owls to drink tea;
    For he said, "To eat mice
    Is not proper or nice,"
That amiable man of Dumbree.
            —*Edward Lear*

A Knowing Raccoon

There once was a knowing raccoon
Who didn't believe in the moon.
    "Every month—don't you see—
    There's a new one," said he,
"No *real* moon could wear out so soon!"
          —*Mary Mapes Dodge*

A Young Man of Cadiz

There was a young man of Cadiz
Who inferred that life is what it is;
    For he had early learnt,
    If it were what it weren't
It could not be that which it is.
          —*J. St. Loe Strachey*

No Easy Job

To manage to keep up a brain
Is no easy job, it is plain;
    That's why a great many
    Don't ever use any,
Thus avoiding the care and the strain.
          —*Anthony Euwer*

A Large Nose

There was an old man of West Dumpet
Who possessed a large nose like a
      trumpet;
    When he blew it loud,
    It astonished the crowd,
And was heard through the whole of
      West Dumpet.
            —Edward Lear

A Young Lady of Troy

There was a young lady of Troy,
Whom several large flies did annoy;
    Some she killed with a thump,
    Some she drowned at the pump.
And some she took with her to Troy.
            —Edward Lear

Bites Her Oysters

There's a lady in Kalamazoo
Who bites her oysters in two;
    She has a misgiving,
    Should any be living,
They'd raise such a hullabaloo.
            —William Bellamy

The Reverend Henry Ward Beecher

The Reverend Henry Ward Beecher
Called a hen a most elegant creature.
    The hen, pleased with that,
    Laid an egg in his hat,
And thus did the hen reward Beecher!
             —Oliver Wendell Holmes

The Pointed Chin

There was a young lady whose chin
Resembled the point of a pin;
    So she made it sharp,
    And purchased a harp,
And played several tunes with her chin.
               —Edward Lear

Was Meant to Give Trouble

The chin it was meant to give trouble,
Either pimples or dimples or stubble,
      Though some have the gall
      To grow not at all,
While others come triple and double.
                    —*Anthony Euwer*

Lighter Than Cork

There once was a girl of New York
Whose body was lighter than cork.
      She had to be fed
      For six weeks upon lead,
Before she went out for a walk.
                    —*Cosmo Monkhouse*

Thin as a Skewer

There was an old fellow of Clewer,
Whose wife was as thin as a skewer;
      Last night, sad to say,
      She, at eight, "passed away,"
Through the bars of a drain to the sewer.
                    —*Langford Reed*

Disgusted with Life

There was an old person of Fife,
Who was greatly disgusted with life.
    They sang him a ballad,
    And fed him on salad,
Which cured that old person of Fife.
             —*Edward Lear*

An Old Man of Sheerness

There was an old man of Sheerness,
Who invited two friends to play chess,
    But he'd lent all the pieces
    To one of his nieces,
And stupidly lost the address.
             —*Randall Davies*

Kept a Baboon

There was an old man of Khartoum,
Who kept a baboon in his room.
    "It reminds me," he said,
    "Of a friend who is dead."
But he would never tell us of whom.
             —*B. G. Bourchier*

Begged an Ant

Once a grasshopper (food being scant)
Begged an ant some assistance to grant;
    But the ant shook his head,
    "I can't help you," he said,
"It's an uncle you need, not an ant."
                    —Oliver Herford

A Puppy

A puppy whose hair was so flowing
There really was no way of knowing
    Which end was his head,
    Once stopped me and said,
"Please, sir, am I coming or going?"
          —*Oliver Herford*

An Old Man With a Beard

There was an old man with a beard,
Who said, "It is just as I feared!—
  Two owls and a hen,
  Four larks and a wren,
Have all built their nests in my beard."
                    —*Edward Lear*

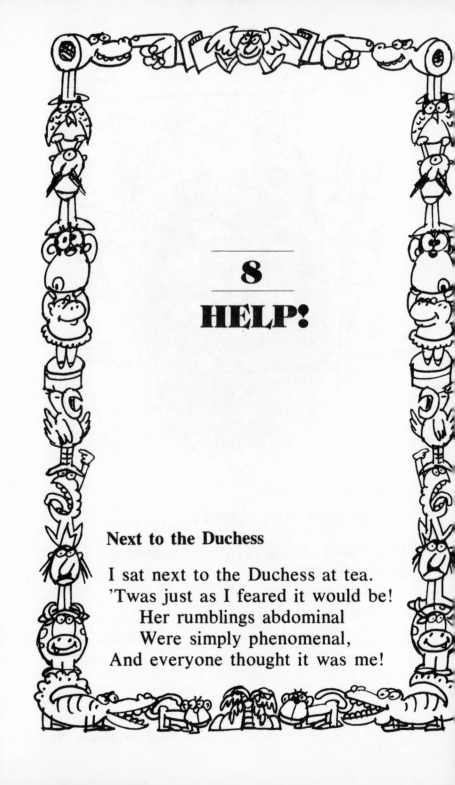

8
HELP!

Next to the Duchess

I sat next to the Duchess at tea.
'Twas just as I feared it would be!
    Her rumblings abdominal
    Were simply phenomenal,
And everyone thought it was me!

Caught in a Flood

A singer they called Miss Diana
Was caught in a flood in Montana.
    She floated away,
    While her beau, so they say,
Accompanied her on the piana.

Caught on Fire

There was a young girl from St. Paul
Wore a newspaper dress to a ball.
    When her dress caught on fire
    It burned her entire
Front page, sporting section, and all!

Call the Doctor!

There once was a boy of Baghdad,
An inquisitive sort of a lad,
    Who said, "I will see
    If a sting has a bee."
Call the doctor! (He found that it had.)

A Luckless Church Tenor

A luckless church tenor was Horace
Whose skin was so terribly porous,
    Sometimes in the choir
    He'd start to perspire,
And nearly drown out the whole chorus.

Never Look Down

There was a young girl from Mobile,
Who went up in a great Ferris Wheel.
    When halfway around,
    She looked down at the ground;
And it cost her a five-dollar meal.

Fond of Grilled Bones

Erasmus Emanuel Jones
Was awfully fond of grilled bones.
  After eating a score,
  He asked for some more—
That's why he lies under these stones.

Please, Boa Constrictor

There once was a man who said, "Oh,
Please, boa constrictor, let go!
  Don't you think that you can?"
  The snake looked at the man,
And calmly responded, "Why, no!"

A Young Lady of Michigan

There was a young lady of Michigan
To see her I never would wish again.
  She'd gobble ice cream
  Till with pain she would scream,
Then she'd order another big dish again.

Fell Flat

A clumsy young soldier named Tom
Fell flat with a thousand-pound bomb.
    And now up on Mars
    They are saying, "My stars!
Where on earth did you emigrate from?"

Sat in His Lap

There was a young lady named Stella
Fell in love with a bow-legged fella.
   The venturesome chap
   Let her sit in his lap
And she fell down clean through to the
   cella.

Fell Down Five Flights

A dizzy old fellow named Topping
Once fell down five flights without
     stopping.
    The janitor swore
    As old Top hit the floor,
"It'll take me the whole darn day
     mopping."

Look Away!

There was a young lady named May
Who played with her false teeth all day.
    When they fell on her plate
    She call out, "I hate
Mithhapth of thith kind! Look away!"

She Was Padded

There was a young lady named Jo
Who was padded from head to her toe.
    She was hit by a truck
    Which was very bad luck—
She's still bouncing, as far as we know.

Fell Down a Sewer

There was a young fellow named Clyde,
Who fell down a sewer and died.
    Now, he had a brother
    Who fell down another,
Would you call that double sewer-side?

Walked with Sister

A talkative fellow named Lister
Went walking one day with his sister.
    A bull at one poke
    Tossed her into an oak,
And 'twas six weeks before Lister missed
      her.

A Bath That She Took

There once was a lady named Harris,
That nothing would ever embarrass,
    Till the powder she shook
    In the bath that she took
Turned out to be plaster of Paris.

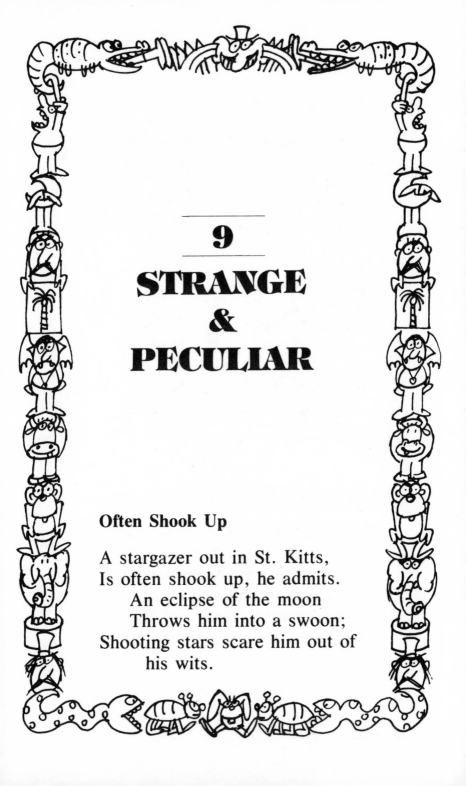

9
STRANGE
&
PECULIAR

Often Shook Up

A stargazer out in St. Kitts,
Is often shook up, he admits.
  An eclipse of the moon
  Throws him into a swoon;
Shooting stars scare him out of
his wits.

A Spaceman Named Dwight

There once was a spaceman named
  Dwight
Whose speed was much faster than light.
  He set out one day,
  In a relative way,
And came back the previous night.

Never Walks Straight

There is an old fellow from Bath,
Who never walks straight down a path.
    You would probably think
    He had too much to drink,
But it's only a way that he hath.

Hauled Out a Crab

A fisherman fishing at Mayfair,
Hauled out a crab who said "Hey,
    there!"
    Some things, it would seem,
    Are removed from the stream
That would have done better to stay
    there.

Have You Heard?

Have you heard of the baby of yore?
Well, no one knew what it was for,
    And being afraid
    It might be mislaid,
They put it away in a drawer.

That Old Peculiar Feeling

There was a young lady of Wheeling
Who had a peculiar feeling
    That she was a fly,
    And she wanted to try
To walk upside down on the ceiling.

No Person Would Dare

There was an old lady of Rye,
With a terrible look in her eye.
    No person would dare
    To respond to her stare,
Or taste her hot blueberry pie!

A Duck's Complaint

A duck whom I happened to hear
Was complaining quite sadly, "Oh, dear!
    Our picnic's today
    But the weathermen say
That the skies will be sunny and clear."

Reeled In a Mermaid

There was an old man of Cape May
Who reeled in a mermaid one day.
    He said, "She's a queen!
    But you should have seen
The one I threw back in the bay!"

Three Little Birds In a Wood

There were three little birds in a wood,
Who always sang hymns when they
    could.
    What the words were about
    They could never make out,
But they felt it was doing them good.

Insisted He'd Sing

A terrible tenor named Bing,
One evening insisted he'd sing.
    So we asked him to stoop,
    Put his head in a loop,
And pulled at each end of the string.

A Sneaky Young Lady

A sneaky young lady of Lynn
Was so unbelievably thin,
    That there was no knowing
    Her coming or going—
And she'd never tell where she'd been!

A Housewife Called Out

A housewife called out with a frown,
When surprised by some callers from
    town,
    "In a minute or less,
    I'll slip on a dress"—
But she slipped on the stairs and came
    down.

An Old Man in a Hearse

There was an old man in a hearse,
Who murmured, "This might have been
    worse.
    Of course, the expense
    Is simply immense,
But it doesn't come out of my purse."

An Old Woman of Honiton

There was an old woman of Honiton,
Whose conduct I've written a sonnet on.
    With a cold in her head,
    She departed to bed
For a week, with her boots and her
    bonnet on.

An Old Kangaroo

There once was an old kangaroo,
Who painted his children sky-blue.
    When his wife said, "My dear,
    Don't you think they look queer?"
He said, "Quiet, or next will be you!"

10
CRAZY?
MAYBE...

Found a New Kind of Disease

There once were some learned
    MD's,
Who found a new kind of disease.
    They bottled and hawked it,
    And then they uncorked it
So thousands could catch it
    with ease.

A Plesiosaurus

There once was a plesiosaurus
Which lived when the earth was all
    porous.
    But it fainted with shame
    When it first heard its name,
And departed long ages before us.

Said What She Meant

There was a young lady of Kent,
Who always said just what she meant.
    People said, "She's a dear—
    So direct—so sincere—"
And they shunned her by common
    consent.

His Old Chewing Gum

A young engine driver at Crewe
Put his old chewing gum in the flue.
    A boy standing by
    Said, "Now I know why
The engine says, "Chew-chew,
    chew-chew!"

Arty McCarty

Did you hear about Arty McCarty?
He sent out the cards for a party.
    But so snooty and few
    Were the people he knew,
That no one was there but poor Arty.

An Old Lady of Brooking

There was an old lady of Brooking,
Who had a great genius for cooking.
   She could bake sixty pies
   All about the same size
And tell which was which without
     looking.

Passion for Truth

There was a young lady named Ruth,
Who had a great passion for truth.
      She said she would die
      Before she would lie,
And she died in the prime of her youth.

An Envious Ermine

"There is," said an envious ermine,
"One thing I just cannot determine:
      When some girl wears my coat,
      She's a person of note;
When I wear it, they call me vermin!"

The Old Math

There was an old man who said, "Do
Tell me how I'm to add two and two.
      It may not be more
      Than just 3 or 4—
But I fear that is rather too few."

The Ice Was Thin

A man and his ladylove, Min,
Skating out where the ice was quite
    thin,
      Had a quarrel, no doubt,
      For I hear they fell out.
It is lucky they didn't fall in!

'Twas Pneumonia

A fellow from Nome with a cough
Would snicker and snortle and scoff
      At warm woolen drawers
      When going outdoors—
'Twas pneumonia that carried him off.

The Countess of Bray

You all know the Countess of Bray,
And you'll hardly believe when I say,
      That in spite of her station,
      Birth, rank, education,
She always spells "cat" with a "k".

Encountered a Puma

A Boston boy went out to Yuma
And there he encountered a puma—
    And later they found
    Just a spot on the ground,
And a puma in a very good huma.

A Young Lady Named Flo

There was a young lady named Flo,
As fat as a capital "O."
    When the people said, "Why
    Is this thus?" She'd reply,
"I suppose it's the way that I grow."

A New Popular Song

There was a composer named Bong,
Who composed a new popular song.
　　It was simply the croon
　　Of a lovesick baboon,
With occasional thumps on the gong.

A Young Lady of Wales

There was a young lady of Wales,
Who wore her hair back in two tails,
　　And the hat on her head
　　That was striped black and red,
Was studded with ten-penny nails.

Writing Right

Said a boy to his teacher one day,
"Wright has not written 'rite' right, I
　　say!"
　　And the teacher replied
　　As the error she eyed:
"Right!—Wright, write 'rite' right, right
　　away!"

A Lively Young Fisher

A lively young fisher name Fisher
Once fished from the edge of a fissure.
   A fish with a grin
   Pulled the fisherman in.
Now they're fishing the fissure for
   Fisher.

11
YOU ASKED FOR IT!

Met a Lion

A handsome young noble of Spain,
Met a lion one day in the rain.
    He ran in a fright
    With all of his might,
But the lion, he ran with his mane!

A Gentleman from Waterloo

A gentleman from Waterloo
Had nothing whatever to do.
    He sat on the stairs
    And counted his hairs,
And found he had seventy-two.

Phineas Fly

A fellow named Phineas Fly
Lived right in a muddy pigsty.
    If you asked why this was,
    He'd reply, "Oh, because—
It's none of your business, that's why!"

The Words She Let Pass

I met a girl once in Savannah,
Who slipped on a peel of banana.
    The words she let pass
    As she fell on the grass,
Would not please her poppa or mamma.

An Old Lady of Herm

There was an old lady of Herm,
Who tied bows on the tail of a worm.
    Said she, "You look festive,
    But don't become restive,
You'll wriggle 'em off if you squirm."

On the Banks of the Nile

A jolly young artist named Bruno
Went to sketch in the bright month of
    June-o
    On the banks of the Nile
    Where a huge crocodile
Quickly tucked him away in his—
    you know!

Too Much Zest

There was a young man from the West
Who loved a young girl with much zest.
    So hard did he press her
    To make her say, "Yes, sir,"
He broke three cigars in his vest.

It Bothered Her Not

There was an old teacher, Miss May,
Whose brain had begun to give way.
    Pupils' names she forgot,
    But that bothered her not,
For she simply addressed them as
       "Hey!"

A Loony Young Lady

A loony young lady, Lucille,
When asked if her hair was for real,
    Replied with a shrug,
    "Just give it a tug,
And judge by the way that I squeal."

She Ate Green Apples

There once was a blushing young bride,
Of eating green apples she died.
   Within the lamented,
   The apples fermented,
Making cider inside her inside.

A Fat Man

There was a fat man in Brookline
Who was asked at what hour he'd dine.
   He replied, "At eleven,
   Four, six, three, and seven.
Not to mention a quarter to nine."

Miss Hyacinthe Gladys McGee

Miss Hyacinthe Gladys McGee
Said somewhat explosively: "Whee!
   If the butt of my back
   Were to sit on a tack,
Think of how pained I should be!"

A Monk's Tale

Said a monk, as he swung by his tail,
To the little monks, female and male:
    "From your offspring, my dears,
    In not-so-many years,
May evolve a professor at Yale!"

God's Plan

God's plan made a hopeful beginning
But man spoiled his chances by sinning.
    We must trust that the story
     Will end in God's glory,
But right now the other side's winning.

A Boy Named Gustave

There once was a boy named Gustave,
Who said that a chimp he must have,
    But his parents said not,
    'Cause they'd already got
All the ape they could take in Gustave.

An Artist Named Fink

An artist named Theodore Fink
Enjoyed making copies in ink.
    Why, the copy he wrote
    Of a five-dollar note
Was so good he is now in the clink.

The Bottle of Perfume

The bottle of perfume that Willie sent
Was highly displeasing to Millicent.
    Her thanks were so cold,
    They quarrelled, I'm told,
Through that silly scent Willie sent
    Millicent.

A Blue Ostrich

An ostrich who lived at the zoo
Was feeling uncomfortably blue.
    So he stuck his whole head
    In the sand in his shed,
"It's not fun, but it's something to
        do . . ."
                —*Sheila Anne Barry*

A Farmer Once Said

A farmer I knew once said, "How
Shall I manage to carry my cow?
    For if I should ask it
    To get in my basket,
I think it would make a big row."

Too Much Soda

There once was a maiden named Rhoda,
Who drank many bottles of soda,
    She slurped so much fizz—
    Well, it's none of my biz—
But one day it's gonna explode-a.

Never on Monday

There once was a cow named Judy
Who now and again was moody.
    She'd give milk on Sunday
    But never on Monday.
What a funny conception of duty!
        —*Barbara Rice*

Call Her Maria (Mar-EYE-ah)

An opera star they called Maria
Tried to sing higher and higher,
    Till she hit a high note
    Which got stuck in her throat—
And she entered the Heavenly Choir.

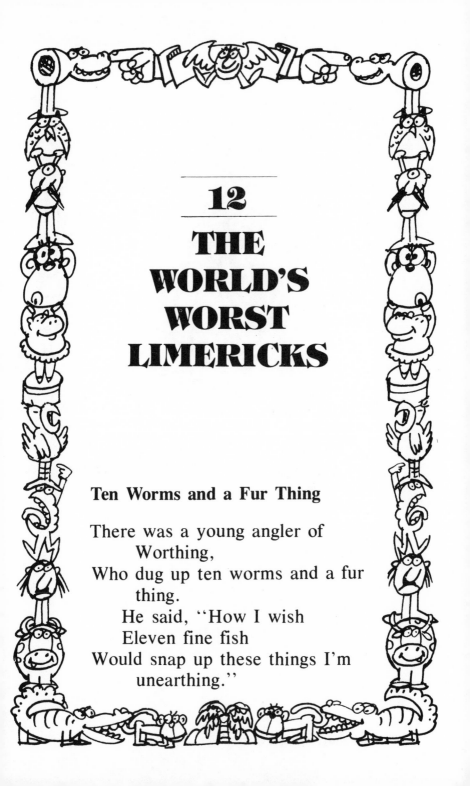

12

THE WORLD'S WORST LIMERICKS

Ten Worms and a Fur Thing

There was a young angler of
    Worthing,
Who dug up ten worms and a fur
    thing.
    He said, "How I wish
    Eleven fine fish
Would snap up these things I'm
    unearthing."

He Couldn't Bring Pets

A vampire—for generations—
Would visit at southern plantations.
    When told with regrets
    That he couldn't bring pets,
He replied, "All my bats are relations!"

A Gent from Florida

A handsome young gent down in Florida
Collapsed in a hospital corridor.
    A young nurse named Krupp
    Tried lifting him up
But dropped him. Now what could be
    horrider?

Just Fine

There was a young fellow from China
Whose feeling for verse was divine-a.
    He thought it just fine
    To end the last line
Quite suddenly.

Went to the Movies

Went to the movies, alack!
Took a front seat in the back.
    Fell down—ah, me—
    From the top balcony
And broke a big bone in my back.

Chiggers and Fleas

A sailor from near Lake Louise
Was so bitten by chiggers and fleas,
    He applied kerosene
    And set fire to his skin (skeen).
He's sailing now over the trees!

A Young Dandy of Butte

There was a young dandy of Butte,
Who sported a bright purple suit.
    When they said, "It's too loud,"
    He answered them, "How'd
I look in a suit that is mute?"

In the Caribbean

There was a young fellow with zest
Who strolled on the pier at Key West.
    He liked being seen
    In the Caribbean
And never cared a bean for the rest.

The Bear Did the Rest

Endeavored a lady in No. Dak.
To shoot a large bear with a Kodak.
    The button she pressed—
    The bear did the rest;
The lady stopped running in So. Dak.

Splashed in the Ocean

There once was a lass from Revere,
So enormously large that, oh, dear!
    When she splashed in the ocean,
    She caused such commotion,
The waves made two ships disappear!

An Old Glutton Named Sam

There was an old glutton named Sam
Who had a great weakness for ham;
    When they brought him bacon,
    He said, "You're mistaken,
But I'll eat it all—pig that I am!"

She Was Peeved

She was peeved and called him "Mr."
Not because he went and kr.,
    But because, just before,
    As she opened the door,
This same Mr. kr. sr.

A Pony from Gorse

There once was a pony from Gorse
Who said to his doctor, "Of course,
    From your bill take half off;
    For you've not cured my cough,
I still find I'm a—little hoarse."

A Shocking Young Lady

There was a young lady of Claridge
Who shocked everyone at her marriage.
    She zoomed down on skates
    To the parish church gates,
While the bridegroom arrived in a
      carriage.

Kick Yourself Hard

"The next time you make up a pun,"
A father once said to his son,
    "Go out in the yard
    And kick yourself hard,
And I will begin when you've done."

INDEX